THE PASSION PUZZLE

DISCOVERING YOUR LIFE'S MISSING PIECE

JAMES BECTON

FORWARD

In the grand tapestry of existence, each of us is like a single thread, weaving our own unique story. At times, this thread may feel frayed or lost, as if searching for its place within the larger design. We yearn for a sense of purpose, a missing piece that would bring meaning to our daily journey.

"The Passion Puzzle: Discovering Your Life's Missing Piece" is a map for those who embark on this quest. It invites you to explore the very essence of your being, to uncover the hidden passions that lie dormant within. This book is not just a guide; it's a revelation, a journey into the heart of what truly matters in life.

We often think of passion as an elusive, all-encompassing force that must be discovered through grand gestures or epic adventures. But the truth is, passion resides within the ordinary moments of our lives. It's in the mundane tasks, the childhood dreams, the quiet whispers of the heart. This book will teach you to see the extraordinary every day.

As you delve into its pages, you will encounter questions—simple yet profound—that will lead you to the core of your being. Questions like, "What would you do if money didn't exist?" and "What kind of superhero are you?" These inquiries will unravel the layers of your identity, revealing the passions that have always been there, waiting to be acknowledged.

Passion is not a distant destination; it's a journey of self-discovery and self-acceptance. It's about embracing your quirks, your talents, and your desires, and allowing them to guide you towards a life of fulfillment and contentment. The journey may not always be smooth, but it will be uniquely yours, and therein lies its beauty.

"The Passion Puzzle" is not just a book; it's a mirror reflecting the untapped potential within you. It's a flashlight that will illuminate the path to your true self. It's a gentle nudge, urging you to live a life aligned with your passions.

As you embark on this journey, remember that you are not alone. Countless others have walked similar paths, facing their fears, embracing their passions, and finding purpose in the everyday. Their stories, shared within these pages, will inspire, and reassure you that the pursuit of passion is a universal endeavor.

So, my dear reader, I invite you to open this book with an open heart and an eager spirit. Allow its wisdom to seep into your soul, guiding you towards a life of authenticity and fulfillment. Your passion is waiting to be discovered, and the missing piece of your life's puzzle is eager to find its place.

May this book be your trusted companion on this remarkable journey. May it empower you to uncover the passions that have always been a part of you. And may it lead you to a life filled with purpose, joy, and the profound satisfaction of knowing that you are living your truth.

Your journey begins now, and the world eagerly awaits the unique tapestry you will weave with the threads of your passions.

TABLE OF CONTENTS

INTRODUCTION

As we journey through the maze of life, where every twist and turn echoes with questions about our purpose, we often find ourselves in relentless pursuit of that elusive element that will infuse our existence with meaning—passion. It is a lifelong journey to discover the holy grail of what sets our souls on fire. If you've ever ventured on this path, you understand the exasperation and obsession that comes with it.

But what if, my friend, it need not be this way? What if passion isn't a rare gem buried deep within but an ember already glowing in your life, waiting to burst into flames? Sounds intriguing, doesn't it?

In the chapters that follow, we'll go on a quest to uncover the passion in the life you're already living. We'll start with the simple yet profound premise that you already have passion in your life. The trick is simply to reveal it, nurture it, and let it seep into every facet of your daily life, from your work to your relationships. Reading this book is your gateway to self-discovery.

How to Use This Guide

First, let's set the stage.

This book will act as both your lantern in the darkness and the roadmap to uncover your passions. Here's how to make the most of this guide:

1. **Read with an Open Heart**: Approach this journey with an open heart and an open mind. Let go of any preconceived notions about what passion should be and allow your journey to unfold.

2. **Reflect and Take Action**: This guide is not a passive read. It's a call to action. As you read each chapter, reflect on the questions and exercises provided. These are your tools for self-discovery and transformation.

3. **Embrace the Process**: Finding your passions isn't an instant revelation. It's a process that takes time. Embrace the journey, and don't be discouraged by occasional detours, as they often lead to the most profound discoveries.

4. **Share and Connect**: You're not alone on this journey. Share your thoughts and experiences with others. Seek out the wisdom of friends, mentors, and fellow travelers. You'll be amazed by the insights and inspiration others can offer.

5. **Enjoy the Adventure**: Above all, remember that this is an adventure. It's a quest filled with surprises, challenges, and moments of pure joy. Enjoy every step of the way.

The Lifelong Search for Purpose

Life is, to many, a profound expedition in search of passion. It is the fervent pursuit of that singular purpose that will breathe meaning into our existence. This journey spans years, often a lifetime, and brims with moments of inspiration, revelation, and deep introspection.

If you've embarked on this quest, you understand its allure and likely have dreams of uncovering that one true thing that sets your soul on fire. Yet, amid the splendor of this expedition, there's a persistent frustration, a shadow looming over you.

For within the quest lies the pressure to find a solitary passion, the "one thing" that will light the way to ultimate fulfillment. A singular purpose that, when found, will bring clarity, and transform life's mismatched mosaic into a masterpiece.

The Frustration of Passion-Seeking

It's important to realize that the path to passion is far from straightforward, and it can be incredibly daunting and all-consuming. It's easy to become disoriented, feeling as if you're lost in a dense forest with no clear way out.

The frustration of this quest lies not in its significance but in the myths and expectations that we indeed have "one true calling," a grand purpose that will define us. This singular view of passion can lead to self-doubt, for if you haven't unearthed your one passion, isn't your life unfulfilling?

In this book, we will delve into passion's complexities and seek to understand why this journey is so crucial for personal growth and fulfillment. We will unravel the mystery of what drives us to find our passion and how this pursuit can lead us to a richer, more meaningful life.

Moreover, we will confront the frustration that often accompanies this journey and examine the very essence of what it means to be passionate. By dissecting the sources of this frustration, we will illuminate our path forward.

As we traverse this terrain of discovery, know that your quest is neither singular nor solitary. It's a multifaceted journey, and this book is your compass to navigate its depths, understand its significance, and find solace in the challenges it presents.

So, are you ready? Take a deep breath, open your heart, and let's start exploring the passions that are waiting to transform your life.

Key Takeaways

- The journey to find your passion is a lifelong quest filled with moments of inspiration, revelation, and introspection.

- The quest for passion is not solitary or straightforward; it's a multifaceted journey.

- This book serves as your compass to navigate the complexities of the quest for passion to understand its significance and find solace in its challenges.

CHAPTER ONE

PASSION IN EVERYTHING YOU DO

The Power of Everyday Passion

Our lives are made up of routines, responsibilities, and countless interactions. It's easy to fall into a pattern of monotony and see each day as a repeat of the last. But what if I told you that within this ordinary framework, you could find extraordinary passion?

Consider the small joys you experience each day, such as savoring your morning coffee, the comforting embrace of a loved one, or the satisfaction of a well-cooked meal (shout out to my wife, Talondia). These seemingly mundane moments carry within them the seeds of passion. They hold the potential to make each day a masterpiece, filled with purpose and meaning.

So how do you recognize these moments when they arise? How do you infuse passion into them? It starts with asking the right questions. One of the most important questions is this:

What Are You Willing to Go Through to Get Ahead?

This question might sound unusual when discussing passion in everyday life, but it's essential to figure out your answer. Just as every rose has its thorns, every aspect of life, no matter how routine or ordinary, has its challenges. Instead of focusing solely on the best parts of your day, pause and reflect on the worst things you're willing to endure.

Consider taking out the garbage, for instance. It's a task many find unpleasant. Yet, what if you approached it with a different mindset? What if you made it your passion to ensure that even the most mundane chores were executed flawlessly?

Surprisingly, finding passion in such places is not unheard of. Take "Waste Connections," a company dedicated to waste management, for example. These professionals have found their passion in an area that many consider unremarkable. Their commitment to maintaining cleanliness, order, and sustainability in our communities is admirable.

This approach might seem unconventional, but it illustrates that passion can be uncovered where you least expect it. When you're willing to go the extra mile even in tasks you find unlikable, you'll be amazed by the passion and satisfaction you can extract from them.

What Was Your Favorite Kind of Day as a Child?

Our childhoods hold the key to understanding our long-lost passions. Think back to the days when you were a wide-eyed dreamer, when the world was full of possibilities and wonder. What kind of activities did you do the most? What brought you the purest joy?

These early memories often contain clues to your present desires. The dreams you held as a twelve-year-old may well align with your current aspirations. Perhaps you spent hours drawing and now find solace in creating art. Or maybe you loved solving puzzles, and today, you excel at troubleshooting complex problems in your career.

By revisiting the past, you can reignite the fires of youthful passion. These interests from your early days can inspire new, purposeful directions in your life today.

What's Easy to Do?

We all possess certain innate abilities, things we do effortlessly and naturally. These skills and talents might seem trivial or commonplace to us, but they are the very essence of our passions. Take a moment to reflect on what you've always found easy.

This could be your knack for playing a musical instrument, your talent for gardening, or even your remarkable memory of people's names. Don't underestimate the significance of these abilities, as they all carry the potential for passion.

Passion doesn't always require a grand quest or a complete career change. Sometimes, it's hidden in plain sight in the form of the things we've always done effortlessly.

In the upcoming chapters, we'll delve deeper into each of these questions to unlock the power of everyday passion. Your life's ordinary moments are woven with potential, and by recognizing the passion within them, you can transform the ordinary into the extraordinary, one day at a time.

Key Takeaways

- Extraordinary passion can be found within the ordinary routines and moments of daily life.

- Small joys, like savoring morning coffee or sharing a meal, carry the seeds of passion and can infuse each day with purpose and meaning.

- Your childhood holds the key to understanding your long-lost passions. Revisit the activities that brought you joy as a child to reignite youthful passions.

CHAPTER TWO

EMBRACING UNCONVENTIONAL PASSION

What Are You Willing to Go Through to Get Ahead?

This is a question that often remains undiscussed. We're used to seeking the best parts of our day that bring us joy and satisfaction, but what about the other side of the coin? What about the tasks that might not make for pleasant conversation? We will explore this next in our quest for passion.

Passion in Unlikely Places

Passion is a chameleon. It doesn't adhere to rigid conventions or predictable paths. To uncover passion's full spectrum, we must open our minds to the unconventional.

Passion is an equal-opportunity force. It doesn't discriminate based on your preconceived notions or society's norms. It thrives where you

5

least expect it, often in the uncharted territories of your life. In the upcoming section, we'll take a look at some real-life stories of individuals who uncovered their passions in the most unlikely of spots.

Their stories are a testament to the idea that passion knows no boundaries. Immerse yourself in these narratives and appreciate the extraordinary diversity of human passions and the myriad ways they can shape a life. We'll start by revisiting an earlier example in more depth.

Waste Connections and the Art of Unconventional Passion

The stench was overwhelming, and the sight was hardly a feast for the eyes. The Waste Connections facility was not on anyone's list of dream workplaces, yet there was a group of employees who looked forward to coming to work each day. These weren't your typical sanitation workers; they were passionate about what they did.

In the bowels of waste management were individuals who had discovered a unique kind of passion. They took pride in waste disposal, an act most would deem unenviable. Yet, it was here that they felt the sweet satisfaction of making the world a cleaner, more orderly place. The unlikely heroes of hygiene taught us a vital lesson: passion knows no boundaries.

Challenging the Conventional

Conventional wisdom often dictates that passion is something you find in established, well-trodden paths. A lifelong passion for teaching, medicine, or the arts, for instance. While these are undoubtedly legitimate sources of passion, limiting yourself to conventional avenues might mean missing out on extraordinary opportunities.

Sometimes, embracing unconventional passion involves a radical departure from the well-worn trail. It might require you to venture into the unfamiliar, the unexplored, or even the eccentric. It's about questioning the traditional boundaries of passion and allowing yourself to be drawn toward what truly ignites your soul.

Consider Angela, a successful lawyer who seemed to have it all: a thriving career, financial stability, and societal approval. But within the confines of her corporate law firm, Angela felt a gnawing emptiness. It wasn't until she followed her curiosity about animal behavior and started volunteering at an animal shelter that she realized her deep passion for animal welfare. Her path shifted dramatically, and she eventually founded her animal rescue organization.

Angela's story is a reminder that sometimes you must be willing to discard the conventional and venture into the unexpected to discover a profound passion that could reshape your life. Embracing the unconventional means being open to unforeseen opportunities and being ready to take risks.

The Diversity of Passion

Passion is not confined to any specific career, hobby, or age group. Passion can be found in all walks of life, whether you're a corporate executive, an artist, a homemaker, or an adventurer. These unconventional passions reveal the rich tapestry of human experience.

Tim was a seasoned accountant with a fascination for the cosmos. He found solace in stargazing, a pursuit he thought was at odds with his career. Yet, in this seemingly unconventional interest, he discovered a passion that illuminated his life in ways his accounting books never could. Tim started volunteering at a local observatory, sharing his love for the stars with curious minds.

Through Tim's story and many others, we begin to understand that our passions are not determined by societal norms or expectations. They're uniquely our own. They don't discriminate based on age, background, or occupation.

A Life Among the Lilies

Lily's journey began with a simple backyard garden, but it quickly grew into something extraordinary.

As a child, Lily had always loved playing in the garden. The feel of the earth between her fingers, the scent of blooming flowers, and the songs of chirping birds were the treasures of her youth. Yet, life had taken her far from these childhood passions and delivered her into the corporate world.

After years of chasing conventional success, Lily yearned for something more. She returned to her childhood oasis and began gardening with renewed vigor. She soon realized that she could turn this passion into a thriving business. Today, Lily's landscaping company has transformed countless dull backyards into lush paradises, and she's found her calling in the petals of her plants.

Maggie's Healing Garden

Maggie, a nurse in a bustling urban hospital, never thought her passion would be gardening. She spent her days tending to patients and her nights nurturing her plants. For her, the hospital's rooftop garden was a sanctuary where she could escape the sterile, fluorescent-lit hallways. Maggie's passion for gardening transformed her into the hospital's unofficial "green thumb guru."

Her daily encounters with illness and suffering made her appreciate the healing power of nature. Patients often accompanied her to the garden, and she saw firsthand the solace it brought them. What began as a personal refuge grew into a beautiful haven for patients seeking respite from their ailments.

Maggie's unconventional passion for gardening evolved into a holistic approach to healthcare, combining the art of healing with the wonders of nature. She proved that passion could thrive even in the most unlikely of environments, making a hospital garden a place of hope, recovery, and comfort.

The Musician with a Song in His Heart

Liam's story is a testament to the magic of street art, as it was in the bustling heart of the city that Liam found his passion as a busker. With his guitar and a voice that could melt hearts, he took to the streets to share his music.

His performances weren't just about earning a living; they were passionate acts of sharing joy with the world. Liam's songs became a backdrop to countless love stories, moments of reflection, and even spontaneous dance sessions. His guitar case overflowed with heartfelt notes of gratitude.

In the seemingly unconventional life of a street musician, Liam found his purpose, bringing joy to countless lives and leaving an indelible mark on the bustling cityscape.

Dive Deep with Professor Ocean

Professor Ocean, as his students fondly called him, was an unassuming marine biology teacher in a landlocked town. Upon seeing the sea for the first time in his forties, it had been love at first sight.

He transformed his landlocked classroom into an underwater world of wonder. His unconventional passion for marine life led him to share the ocean's mysteries with students who had never even glimpsed the sea. His enthusiasm was infectious, and soon, he had a group of young marine biologists eager to explore a world they had only read about.

Professor Ocean's story reminds us that passion isn't restricted by geography. You can dive deep into your calling, even if it seems oceans away. It's about the depth of your commitment, not your proximity to what you love.

These stories are just the beginning. The world is filled with countless more examples of unconventional passions that defy stereotypes and inspire us to look beyond the obvious. By recognizing these narratives, we open our minds to the extraordinary diversity of passions that exist in the world. Each story is a testament to the idea that passion is not confined by conventions; it's about what sets your soul on fire.

Embracing Your Unconventional Passions

So, how do you begin to explore the realm of unconventional passions? It starts with an open mind and a willingness to ask yourself what truly piques your interest. Think beyond what's expected or typical. Consider hobbies, activities, or ideas you've dismissed because they didn't fit the mold.

Take a moment to reflect on those fleeting moments when you felt a spark of enthusiasm, whether it was designing board games or experimenting with a new recipe. These moments could be the seeds of your undiscovered passions.

It's also important to be open to new experiences. Attend events or gatherings that align with your unique interests. Engage in conversations with people from different walks of life.

You never know where your next passion may be lurking.

Key Takeaways

- Passion can thrive in unlikely places and unconventional pursuits, challenging preconceived notions of what ignites the soul.

- Unconventional passions often involve stepping away from well-trodden paths, embracing the unexpected, and taking risks.

- Diversity is the hallmark of passion; it transcends age, background, or occupation, demonstrating that it is uniquely personal and not bound by societal norms

CHAPTER THREE

A GLIMPSE INTO YOUR CHILDHOOD

Your Favorite Kind of Day as a Child

Think back to your childhood. Close your eyes for a moment and let the memories wash over you. What were your favorite days like? The ones that made your heart sing and filled you with excitement from the moment you woke up. Those were the days when passion began to take root within you, even if you didn't realize it at the time.

For some, it was the simple joy of running through sprinklers on a hot summer day. The feeling of water droplets on their skin, the laughter of friends echoing in the background. For others, it might have been the crisp, cool days of autumn when the world turned into a vibrant canvas of reds and yellows. Perhaps you were the kind of child who loved curling up with a good book, lost in fantastical worlds for hours on end.

Our childhood days often held a sense of freedom and wonder that can be challenging to recapture in the busyness of adulthood. But within those days lie the seeds of our passions. These early experiences, driven by pure curiosity and unbridled joy, can provide invaluable clues about the passions you might be neglecting in your adult life.

Seeds of Passion from Your Youth

Our childhood dreams are like tiny treasures buried within us. They might not have been fully formed or even particularly practical, but they were sincere. Whether it was your dream of becoming an astronaut, an artist, a teacher, or even a superhero, those dreams carried the essence of your true self.

As adults, we often abandon or forget these early aspirations. We tuck them away in the corners of our minds, dismissing them as childish fantasies. But what if we were to dust off these dreams, examine them in the light of who we've become, and realize that some part of that childhood dream still resonates with our current desires?

Consider the story of Sarah, a successful corporate executive who had always dreamed of being an archeologist as a child. Her fascination with digging up ancient artifacts in her backyard was the highlight of her youth. Yet, she chose a path that seemed more practical and financially rewarding in business. As the years went by, she felt increasingly unfulfilled, even though she had achieved considerable success in her career.

It wasn't until Sarah decided to volunteer at an archeological site during her vacation that she rediscovered the profound sense of wonder and excitement she felt as a child. The experience rekindled her passion for history and uncovering the past. She realized that her childhood dream had never truly died; it had only been buried beneath layers of adult responsibilities and societal expectations.

I invite you to revisit your own childhood dreams. What did you dream of becoming? What did you love doing more than anything else? What could you spend hours on without ever feeling bored or tired? These questions hold the keys to unlocking the passions that have been with you all along.

It's an eye-opening journey into your past, where you'll find the breadcrumbs leading you to the passions that may have been lying dormant but are ready to flourish once again. As you unearth these seeds of passion from your youth, you'll discover new avenues for fulfillment and purpose that are uniquely yours.

Key Takeaways

- Childhood memories hold the seeds of our passions. Reflecting on your favorite childhood days can reveal what truly makes your heart sing.

- The carefree days of childhood are often filled with curiosity, unbridled joy, and moments of pure wonder, and they contain invaluable clues about the passions you may be neglecting as an adult.

- As adults, we often bury or forget our early aspirations, dismissing them as childish fantasies. However, by reexamining these dreams in the light of who we've become, we might realize that they still resonate with our current desires.

CHAPTER FOUR

THE THINGS YOU FIND EASY

What's Easy to Do?

In our quest for passion and purpose, we often overlook our innate abilities and talents. Therefore, this chapter is about recognizing those skills and tasks that come naturally to you, as they can be powerful indicators of your passions.

We all have something we're good at, something that we excel in without much effort. These are your natural talents. It might be playing a musical instrument, solving complex mathematical problems, connecting with people on a deep level, or even making the perfect cup of coffee. We often take these abilities for granted, thinking that if they come easily to us, they can't be that special. But that's not true.

Recognizing Your Natural Talents

Your natural talents are like compasses guiding you to your passions. They are not random; they are intertwined with your deepest desires and the things that truly matter to you. To understand your passions, you first need to understand these talents.

Let's take a moment to reflect on this. Think about the activities or skills you find easy, almost effortless. It could be something as simple as organizing your workspace or cooking a delicious meal. Maybe you're that person who can defuse tense situations with your calming presence, or perhaps you have a knack for making people laugh.

Remember, no talent is too small or too ordinary. It's often the things we consider unremarkable that can lead us to profound passions. Consider them as the building blocks of your unique path to fulfillment.

But how do you recognize your natural talents? Sometimes, they are so ingrained in your daily life that you might not even notice them. Start by paying attention to the following:

1. **Ease and Enjoyment:** What tasks do you find easy and enjoyable? What activities could you do for hours without getting bored or tired? Your natural talents often align with these effortless tasks.

2. **Compliments and Requests:** What do people around you praise you for? What do they ask for your help with? If your friends always ask for your advice on a specific topic or if your colleagues turn to you to solve particular issues, this is a sign of your unique talent.

3. **Childhood Hobbies:** Sometimes, our childhood hobbies offer profound insights into our natural talents. What did you enjoy doing as a child? Were you drawn to creating things, solving puzzles, or telling stories?

4. **In-the-Zone Moments:** Recall moments when you were so engrossed in an activity that you lost track of time. These "flow" experiences often point to areas where you naturally excel.

5. **Feedback and Self-Reflection:** Don't hesitate to ask for feedback from those who know you well. Sometimes, they can see your talents more clearly than you can. Additionally, self-reflection is a powerful tool. Use it to consider what makes you feel fulfilled and accomplished.

Your talents are unique to you, and they hold the potential to lead you to your passions. However, recognizing them is just the first step. The real magic happens when you start nurturing these abilities and applying them to areas of your life that matter most.

By recognizing your natural talents, you'll not only uncover new avenues of passion but will also gain a deeper understanding of your authentic self. As you move forward in your journey, remember that your talents are not meant to be hidden; they are your gifts to share with the world.

Key Takeaways

- Your natural talents are like a compass guiding you toward your passions. Don't underestimate the skills and tasks that come easily to you; they hold the keys to your fulfillment.

- Recognize your natural talents by paying attention to what tasks you find easy and enjoyable, what others praise you for, your childhood hobbies, moments of "flow," and self-reflection.

- Recognizing your natural talents isn't enough; it's essential to use them to lead a life that resonates with your true self and to share your unique gifts with the world.

CHAPTER FIVE

YOUR VALUABLE SKILLS

What Do People Ask You for Help With?

In our ongoing quest to find passion and purpose, sometimes the most valuable clues are right under our noses. Often times, our passions can be found in those tasks or skills others approach you for.

Think about it for a moment. People come to you for help with specific things. It could be your expertise in computers, your knack for interior decorating, or your ability to lead a meeting effectively. These are not coincidences; they are insights into your unique talents and the value you bring to others.

Valuable Skills and Passions

Your skills are like the bridge that connects you to your passions. They represent your natural abilities, honed over time, and are intertwined with the things that make you feel alive.

18

Consider these key points:

1. Valuable Skills Come Naturally: Often, the skills that are in high demand from your friends, family, and colleagues are those that come most naturally to you. You excel in these areas without a second thought. It's as if you have an innate talent for them.

2. Recognizing Valuable Skills is Crucial: Understanding the link between the skills you possess and your passions is crucial for leading a more fulfilling life. These skills can guide you towards your true calling, allowing you to do what you love and contribute meaningfully to the world.

So, how do you identify these skills? Here's a process to help you recognize them:

3. Pay Attention to What People Ask For: Take note of what people often ask you for. Are your friends always asking for your advice on a specific topic? Does your boss consistently turn to you to handle important tasks? These requests are hints at your valuable skills.

4. Reflect on Your Natural Abilities: Consider what you do naturally, things that feel effortless to you. These can be skills like organizing, problem-solving, communication, or any number of other talents. These are your gifts.

5. Consider What You Love to Do: When you think about the tasks or activities you enjoy the most, they often align with your skills. Your passions frequently coincide with what you are good at.

6. Ask for Feedback: Don't hesitate to ask those around you what they think your strengths are. Sometimes, the people who know you best can see your abilities more clearly than you can yourself.

Once you've identified your valuable skills, it's time to make the connection between these skills and your passions. Your skills can be the tools that allow you to pursue what you love most effectively. They enable you to make a meaningful impact and derive immense satisfaction from your pursuits.

In the upcoming chapters, we'll take the next step and explore how to integrate these skills into your daily life. Then, you will not only discover new sources of passion but will also gain a deeper understanding of your authentic self.

Remember, your skills are gifts meant to be shared with the world. They are instrumental in making a difference in your life and others. As you move forward on this journey to a more passionate life, you'll realize that your skills and passions are not separate entities. They are interconnected, and together, they can bring you unparalleled fulfillment.

Key Takeaways

- The tasks and skills that others frequently seek your help with can provide essential clues about your deepest passions.

- Valuable skills often come naturally and effortlessly to you. Recognizing and understanding the link between these skills and your passions is crucial for leading a fulfilling life.

- To identify your valuable skills, pay attention to what people ask for, reflect on your natural abilities, consider what you love to do, and ask for feedback from those who know you well.

CHAPTER SIX

A WORLD WITHOUT MONEY

What Would You Do if Money Didn't Exist?

Money has an undeniable influence on our decisions and pursuits. Often, our choices are driven by the need to earn a living and secure our financial well-being. But what if we could remove the shackles of monetary constraints and explore what we truly desire?

In this chapter, we challenge the conventional wisdom that ties our passions to financial rewards. We dare to envision a world without money, where your actions are not dictated by the size of your paycheck but by the size of your dreams.

Identifying True Desires

Picture a world where the concept of money doesn't exist. You have all you need to lead a healthy, fulfilling life. In this utopian world, what would you do with your time?

When money is no longer a driving force, you can explore your deepest desires without the shadow of financial constraints. This change in perspective can be liberating and revealing. Here's how you can use this thought experiment to identify your true desires:

1. Dismantle Financial Barriers: Begin by removing money from your decision-making process. Forget about the need to pay bills, buy a bigger house, or save for retirement. In this thought experiment, you have everything you need for a content life.

2. Explore Unfiltered Passions: With these constraints gone, consider what activities genuinely excite you. What hobbies, causes, or interests would you pursue purely because they bring you joy and fulfillment?

3. Imagine Your Ideal Day: Create a vivid picture of your perfect day in this money-free world. What would you do from the moment you wake up until you go to bed? Your ideal day reflects your deepest desires.

4. Reflect on Your Childhood Dreams: Revisit the aspirations you had as a child. What did you dream of becoming or achieving when you were young? Often, our childhood dreams contain hints about our authentic desires.

5. Prioritize Personal Growth: Consider how you'd invest in yourself. Would you engage in learning, self-improvement, or skill development? What aspects of personal growth would you pursue?

6. Explore Creative and Artistic Passions: In a world without money, you might find that your artistic or creative passions take center stage. What artistic projects or creative endeavors would you embark on if finances were not a concern?

7. Focus on Impact and Contribution: Think about the positive changes you'd like to make in the world. How would you contribute to your community, society, or the planet? What causes or issues would you passionately support?

8. Embrace Your Inner Entrepreneur: Without the fear of financial risk, would you consider entrepreneurial endeavors? How would you use your skills and talents to create something meaningful for yourself and others?

As you delve into this mental exercise, you may find that your true desires shine through with remarkable clarity. When you're no longer bound by financial considerations, your passions have the freedom to flourish.

It's important to remember that this exercise isn't about dismissing financial responsibility in the real world. It's about discovering what you truly value when money isn't the driving force. By identifying your purest desires, you can then seek ways to incorporate them into your life, even within the constraints of the financial system.

In the upcoming chapters, we'll explore how you can integrate these insights into your daily existence. When you align your actions with your true desires, you unlock the potential for a life that's not only financially rewarding but deeply fulfilling.

So, let your imagination roam freely in this world without money, and in doing so, you might just find the passions and desires that have been waiting to emerge once the financial fog has lifted.

Key Takeaways

- To identify your true desires, mentally remove financial barriers, and consider the activities that genuinely excite you.

- This thought experiment isn't about dismissing financial responsibility but discovering what you truly value when money isn't the driving force.

- When you align your actions with your true desires, you unlock the potential for a life that's not only financially rewarding but deeply fulfilling.

CHAPTER SEVEN

THE JOY OF THE PAST

What Brought You Joy in the Past?

In the whirlwind of our modern lives, it's easy to forget the simple moments of pure, unadulterated joy. Throughout your life, there have been times when your heart raced with excitement, and every second felt like a gift. In this chapter, we're going to dive into the past, rummage through your memories, and uncover the hidden treasures of happiness.

Reflecting on Happy Memories

Happy memories are like stars that guide us through the darkest of nights. They provide illumination, not just about where we've been but where we're going. These are the moments that touched your soul and made you feel truly alive. They also hold vital clues about your passions.

Let's embark on a journey down memory lane. Here's how you can reconnect with your past and excavate passions you might have overlooked:

1. Time Travel in Your Mind: Find a quiet space where you won't be disturbed. Sit or lie down comfortably, close your eyes, and take a few deep breaths to center yourself. Then, let your mind wander to your childhood. Try to recall the moments that made you the happiest. It could be a specific birthday, a family vacation, or just an ordinary day when you felt an extraordinary sense of joy.

2. Visualize the Scene: Once you've summoned a joyful memory, let it play out in your mind like a movie. Imagine the sights, sounds, and even the scents of that moment. Recreate it as vividly as possible. Feel the emotions you experienced during that time. What made it so special?

3. Journal Your Emotions: Now, grab a journal or a piece of paper. Write down the memory you've just revisited. Describe the details, but more importantly, delve into your emotions. What were you feeling at that moment? The thrill of discovery, the warmth of family, the satisfaction of personal achievement—capture it all.

4. Identify the Key Elements: Once you've dissected the memory, identify the key elements that brought you joy. It could be spending time with loved ones, being in nature, creating something, helping others, or learning something new. These are the building blocks of your passions.

5. Connect Past and Present: Now, it's time to bridge the gap between the past and the present. How can you infuse your current life with these elements of joy? If playing in nature filled you with delight, could hiking, gardening, or simply taking a daily walk bring back that joy? If it was creating something, consider a new hobby or a side project. If it was helping others, explore volunteer opportunities.

6. Embrace the Joy: Whatever elements of your joyful past you've identified, don't just let them remain memories. Embrace them as integral parts of your present and future. If you integrate these elements into your life, you can rekindle the happiness you once experienced.

Remember, the purpose of this exercise is not just to dwell on the past but to use it as a source of inspiration. Your past joy is a treasure chest waiting to be unlocked. By revisiting these moments, you gain insights into what truly makes you happy, and from there, you can cultivate passions that infuse your life with meaning. Your journey is a unique one, and these clues from your past are invaluable signposts along the way.

Key Takeaways

- Reflect on joyful memories from your past by taking a mental journey back in time.

- Visualize these moments in detail and capture the emotions you felt during those special times.

- Your past joy is a treasure chest of inspiration waiting to be unlocked, providing insights into what truly makes you happy and guiding you toward passions that infuse your life with meaning.

CHAPTER EIGHT

WHAT KIND OF SUPERHERO ARE YOU?

The World Needs Changing

The world is a vast and complex place. It contains a blend of joy, suffering, hope, and despair, and it's easy to feel overwhelmed. You might wonder, "What can one person do in the face of such enormity?" The truth is, you can do a lot more than you might think.

Superheroes are known for saving the world.

When we think of superheroes, we envision caped crusaders, extraordinary beings with superhuman abilities who swoop in to save the day. But let's step away from the world of comic books and movies for a moment and consider the idea of being a real-life hero.

The Aspects of the World that Need Change

In the vast tapestry of human existence, we often find ourselves facing adversaries just as captivating as those depicted in the legendary stories of superheroes. While these antagonists may not be equipped with diabolical powers or lurk in the shadows wearing sinister costumes, they are formidable adversaries in their own right. In our world, villains often take the form of complex issues like poverty, inequality, environmental degradation, educational disparities, substance abuse, pollution, homelessness, domestic violence, sex trafficking, or mental health stigma.

1. **Poverty**: A relentless adversary that continues to afflict a substantial portion of the global population. Poverty is a pervasive force that denies individuals access to life's basic necessities, such as food, shelter, and education. Its persistence perpetuates a cycle of deprivation, trapping countless people in its grasp.

2. **Inequality**: A multifaceted nemesis that takes many forms. It includes gender inequality, racial disparities, and economic imbalances, all of which curtail countless individual's potential. Inequality is a pervasive force that denies individuals equal opportunities and treatment, creating divisions in society that hinder collective progress.

3. **Environmental Degradation**: An ominous adversary that threatens the very fabric of our planet. The issues encompassed in this adversary are extensive, from climate change and deforestation to pollution and resource depletion. The consequences of environmental degradation are global, affecting ecosystems, communities, and future generations.

4. **Educational Disparities**: A silent adversary that, despite advances in access to education, still denies many the right to quality learning. It perpetuates disparities that limit

opportunities for personal growth, prosperity, and societal development.

5. **Substance Abuse**: A pervasive nemesis that ensnares individuals and communities in the cycle of addiction. Substance abuse brings with it a multitude of personal and societal consequences, leading to suffering, instability, and loss of life.

6. **Pollution**: An insidious adversary that contaminates the very air we breathe, the water we drink, and the soil that sustains us. Pollution poses grave risks to both the environment and human health, making it a challenge that demands our attention and action.

7. **Homelessness**: A pressing and unyielding foe that leaves a significant portion of the world's population without the security of a home. Homelessness is a fundamental human rights issue, as it denies individuals access to shelter, security, and dignity.

8. **Domestic Violence**: A shadowy nemesis that lurks within the confines of homes, shattering lives and communities. Domestic violence is a hidden but pervasive challenge, inflicting physical and emotional harm on victims and perpetuating cycles of abuse.

9. **Sex Trafficking**: A deeply troubling adversary that preys on the vulnerable, exploiting and victimizing individuals in the darkest corners of society. It represents a grave violation of human rights, requiring global efforts to eradicate it.

10. **Mental Health Stigma**: An insidious nemesis that has shrouded discussions of mental health in silence and shame. This adversary prevents individuals from seeking the help and support they need, perpetuating suffering and social isolation.

These are the problems that need solving, and guess what? You have the potential to be a real-world hero, tackling these challenges in your own way. These adversaries, although they may not be tangible villains, demand our attention and action. In this chapter, we delve into the idea that each one of us possesses the potential to become a real-world hero. You don't need to wear a cape or wield superhuman powers; your unique abilities, passion, and dedication are enough.

Uncover Your Inner Superhero

But to be a hero, you need to identify your superpowers. **Every superhero has unique abilities that make them special.** For some, it's super strength or the ability to fly. In your case, it might be your charisma, your problem-solving skills, your creativity, or your determination. We all have something special, something we're exceptionally good at. We call these talents and skills our superpowers.

Let's embark on a journey to uncover your inner superhero:

1. Reflect on Your Strengths: Take a moment to think about the things you're good at, the things that come naturally to you. Are you a great communicator, a skilled negotiator, a compassionate listener, or a brilliant organizer? These are your superpowers.

2. Recognize Your Passions: Now, consider what really fires you up and makes you come alive. It could be teaching, mentoring, caring for the environment, advocating for social justice, or creating beautiful art. Your passions are a compass directing you toward your heroic mission.

3. Identify the Issues: Next, look at the world around you. What issues, problems, or challenges do you feel deeply connected to? Is it the struggle for equality, the need for quality education, the fight against climate change, or something else entirely? These are your adversaries to overcome.

4. **Match Your Superpowers to the Issues:** Once you've identified your superpowers and passions, match them with the issues that tug at your heart. For example, if you're a great communicator and you're passionate about education, you might consider mentoring underprivileged students. If you're a brilliant organizer and care deeply about the environment, you could lead community clean-up efforts.

5. **Define Your Mission:** Your mission as a real-world superhero is unique to you. Define it clearly. Maybe you aim to empower underrepresented communities, protect endangered species, or advance medical research. This mission becomes your purpose.

6. **Take Action:** No superhero just sits around in a lair. They take action. Your mission should inspire you to make a difference. Whether it's volunteering, starting a project, raising awareness, or contributing your skills to a cause, your superpowers can have a real impact.

The world needs changing, and real-life heroes are the ones who lead the way. Your superpowers, combined with your passions, can be a force for good. So, be the hero the world needs, one superpower at a time. Your unique abilities, your passions, and your mission can create ripples of change, and as you'll soon discover, there's no feeling quite like the satisfaction of knowing you've made the world a better place.

Key Takeaways

- While we often think of superheroes as fictional characters with superhuman abilities, you can be a real-life hero by addressing real-world challenges.

- Match your superpowers and passions with the issues that resonate with you, creating a meaningful connection between your abilities and the challenges you wish to overcome.

- Take concrete actions to make a difference, whether through volunteering, initiating projects, raising awareness, or using your skills for a cause you're passionate about.

CHAPTER NINE

LIVING WITH URGENCY

Life, in all its beauty and complexity, is a finite journey. It's a truth we often avoid, sometimes for decades. But when we confront the idea that our time is limited, something remarkable happens. The urgency of living awakens within us, and we begin to focus on what truly matters.

You're Dying. What Do You Want to Do with Your Time Left?

The word "dying" might seem harsh, even inappropriate, but it's a truth we must all come to terms with eventually. Every day is a step closer to the end of our journey. While this might sound morbid, facing the reality of limited time can be incredibly liberating.

Consider for a moment that you've been given a diagnosis, one that provides a definitive but unknown expiration date. Suddenly, life becomes stripped down and simplified. You're no longer preoccupied with trivial matters. Instead, two fundamental questions demand your attention:

1. What do I do next for my health?

- Health takes center stage. Every decision becomes about nourishing your body, mind, and spirit. You're more conscious of what you eat, how you move, and the quality of your sleep. You may seek out holistic practices, explore new forms of exercise, or focus on stress reduction. Your body becomes your temple, and every action is a prayer for health.

2. What do I want to do in case this goes bad?

- Here's where it gets fascinating. It's more than just having a bucket list. This is about defining things that are deeply relevant to you. Suddenly, your life's purpose crystallizes, and the things that matter most stand out brightly, like beacons in the night. Traveling to a distant country, reconciling with an old friend, writing a book, building a charitable foundation—these are no longer distant dreams but immediate imperatives. When time is limited, you want to spend it wisely.

Defining Your Most Important Actions

Now, let's shift our focus back to reality. The truth is, none of us know when our time will run out. However, the essence of urgency remains profoundly relevant.

The urgency of living means doing things now, not someday. It means living deliberately, taking charge of your time, and prioritizing what aligns with your passions. Here's how you can apply this sense of urgency to your life:

1. Clarify Your Priorities: Define your most important actions. What things would make you feel deeply fulfilled if you achieved them? Make a list. Is it spending more time with your family? Advancing your career? Writing a novel? Volunteering for a cause you're passionate about? These are your priorities and guiding stars.

2. Eliminate Distractions: Urgency requires focus. Identify and remove distractions that keep you from your priorities. This might mean cutting down on social media, restructuring your work schedule for greater efficiency, or decluttering your physical space.

3. Set Specific Goals: Urgency thrives on specificity. Define clear, actionable goals related to your priorities. Instead of saying, "I want to travel more," set a goal like, "I will visit three new countries in the next two years." Specific goals are like roadmaps, guiding you to your desired destinations.

4. Take Immediate Action: Procrastination is the enemy of urgency. Start working on your priorities today. Even a small step is progress. If you're passionate about writing, begin your novel's first chapter. If you want to spend more time with your family, schedule a family dinner this week. The key is to act now, for tomorrow is never guaranteed.

5. Practice Gratitude: Urgency often emerges from an appreciation of life's fleeting moments. Ensure you practice gratitude regularly. Reflect on the beauty around you and the people who enrich your life. Gratitude is a profound motivator.

6. Embrace Change: Urgency can lead to transformative change. Be open to new experiences, even if they're outside your comfort zone. Change is a catalyst for growth and the pursuit of your passions.

Remember, urgency isn't about rushing through life. It's about savoring every moment and ensuring that you live authentically, aligned with your deepest passions and desires.

When you wake up each morning, consider that this day might be one of your last. Live with intention. Seize your passions. Define your most important actions and act upon them urgently. Life is precious. Embrace it.

Key Takeaways

- Life is a finite journey, and acknowledging the reality of our limited time can be liberating, pushing us to focus on what truly matters.

- To apply a sense of urgency to your life, clarify your priorities, eliminate distractions, set specific goals, take immediate action, practice gratitude, and embrace change.

CHAPTER TEN

PRIORITIZING YOUR TIME

Time is the most precious thread in our life's tapestry. Each day, we weave our moments, actions, and priorities into a unique pattern that defines our existence. There's no doubt that how we spend our time is important, but how often do we pause to consider where it truly goes?

How Do You Spend Your Time?

Time, that elusive commodity, is like sand slipping through an hourglass. We often say we don't have enough of it, yet the truth is that pockets of free time exist all around us. Therefore, to prioritize our passions, we must first understand how we spend our time.

Consider the hour before you go to bed. This is a pocket of time that often escapes us as we watch TV, scroll through social media, or simply zone out. Then there are those two hours you might have after work. Are they spent productively pursuing your passions, or do they dissolve into nothingness?

Assess Your Time Allocation: No Judgment

There's no judgment here. We all have our guilty pleasures, forms of relaxation, and "just chilling" moments. My aim is not to condemn how you spend your time but to encourage you to examine it.

Take a closer look at your daily routine. What activities do you prioritize? If you're watching TV, ask yourself why. What is it about those shows that draw you in? The truth is that your choices reveal aspects of your interests and passions.

Unveiling Hidden Passions

Passions are often lurking beneath the surface of your daily activities, waiting for you to discover them. It's not about turning your life upside down but about recognizing the potential for passion in your existing routines.

Think about the times when you've been most engaged or felt genuine joy. What were you doing? Was it gardening, cooking, writing, or discussing a particular subject? These moments hold the key to your hidden passions.

The hour you spend talking about a specific book with a friend might indicate a latent love for literature. That time when you were engrossed in a home improvement project could reveal an affinity for design or renovation.

Reflect on Your Daily Choices

As you reflect on your daily choices, remember that your passions don't have to be monumental or require significant time investments.

They can be woven into the fabric of your everyday life.

Suppose you find yourself drawn to cooking during your free time. This might signal a passion for culinary arts. Now consider how you can elevate this passion. Can you experiment with new recipes? Take a cooking class? Share your culinary adventures on a blog or social media?

Or perhaps you lose yourself in the world of books and literature. This is an opportunity to expand your passion by joining a book club, writing reviews, or even penning your own stories.

Embrace Your Passions

In prioritizing your time, the goal is to embrace your passions, both the known and the hidden. It's about recognizing that life is not just a sequence of minutes but a collection of moments filled with meaning and purpose.

Your daily routines, if aligned with your passions, can become a source of fulfillment and joy. As you assess how you spend your time, keep an open heart and mind. Your true passions may be closer than you think, waiting for the moment when you decide to give them the time and attention they deserve.

Key Takeaways

- Time is a precious thread in the tapestry of life. We often claim not to have enough of it, but pockets of free time exist all around us.

- Your daily choices reveal aspects of your interests and passions. What engages you and brings you joy offers insights into your hidden passions.

- Life is not just a sequence of minutes but a collection of moments. Align your daily routines with your passions to weave a tapestry of joy, purpose, and fulfillment.

CHAPTER ELEVEN

DREAMS DEFERRED

Life has a peculiar way of steering us away from our deepest desires. As responsibilities pile up and priorities shift, our dreams often find themselves relegated to the backseat. But here's a question worth pondering: What if those long-forgotten dreams hold the key to our true passions?

Everyone has dreams they've put on hold.

In the cacophony of daily life, it's easy to tuck our dreams away in dusty drawers, thinking we'll revisit them later. We promise ourselves, "Someday, I'll get back to it." It is these very dreams that might be your true passions in disguise.

This chapter is an invitation to dust off those old dreams and to unfold and examine them with a fresh perspective. Start by recalling the aspirations you've tucked away. Maybe it was that novel you always wanted to write, the language you meant to learn, or the travel adventures you envisioned.

Consider why you put these dreams on hold. Life's practicalities might have taken precedence, but understanding the reasons behind your deferred dreams can illuminate what truly matters to you.

The Importance of Your Long-Term Goals

Dreams are often intertwined with long-term goals. These goals, the ones you hope to achieve in the distant future, can offer invaluable insights into your passions. They are like stars on the horizon, guiding your life's journey.

Think about your long-term goals, both the ones you've written down and the ones you've kept in your heart. These are the destinations you're striving for. They can be personal, like achieving a sense of inner peace, or professional, like building a successful business.

Recognizing the Alignment Between Dreams and Long-Term Goals

Now, align these long-term goals with your deferred dreams. Consider how realizing these dreams might lead you closer to your long-term objectives. Maybe that novel you dreamed of writing aligns with your goal to inspire others with your creativity. Learning a new language could enhance your ability to connect with a broader global audience if that's one of your goals.

By recognizing the connections between your deferred dreams and your long-term goals, you can begin to weave the threads of passion back into your life.

Embracing Your Passions Through Dreams

Remember, passions aren't always grandiose or easily identifiable. They can reside in the simplest of dreams, and quiet, subtle yearnings can lead to profound satisfaction.

As you embark on this journey to revisit your deferred dreams, consider what steps you can take today to bring them back into your life. Even small actions like setting aside time each day to write or dedicating an hour a week to learning a new language can reignite your passion.

Your Dreams Are Your True North

Ultimately, the pursuit of your deferred dreams can be a gateway to living a more passionate and fulfilled life. They can serve as your compass, guiding you toward a life that aligns with your deepest desires.

This chapter is a reminder that it's never too late to rekindle your dreams. They are your treasures and potential sources of passion. Your dreams are a testament to your innermost wishes, and they hold the power to infuse your days with purpose and enthusiasm.

As you move forward, consider how embracing these deferred dreams can bring you closer to the passionate life you've always longed for. Sometimes, it's in the pursuit of what we once set aside that we discover the most profound meaning and fulfillment.

Key Takeaways

- Life often leads us away from our deepest desires as responsibilities and priorities accumulate. Long-forgotten dreams might be the keys to our true passions.

- Embrace your passions through your dreams, no matter how simple or subtle they may be. Small, consistent actions such as setting aside time each day to work on your dreams can reignite your passion.

- Your deferred dreams can serve as your compass, guiding you toward a life that aligns with your deepest desires. Rekindling these dreams is never too late, and they hold the power to infuse your days with purpose and enthusiasm.

CHAPTER TWELVE

YOUR FAVORITE STORIES

Stories have an incredible power to touch our hearts and minds. The tales we love, whether on the big screen or in the pages of a book, often hold a mirror to our interests, values, and, yes, even our passions. In this chapter, we'll discuss what your favorite stories reveal about the passions that lie within you.

Your Ten Favorite Movies and Books

Begin by compiling a list of your ten all-time favorite movies and books. These are the stories that you can revisit time and time again without growing weary. It could be the classic novel that never left your side or the movie that you recommend to everyone you meet.

Why Our Favorite Stories Matter

You might be wondering, what do these preferences have to do with passion and purpose? Well, your favorite stories hold a unique key to your inner world. They are not random choices; they reflect the themes and narratives that resonate most deeply with you.

Think about why you love these stories. Is it the hero's journey, the underdog's triumph, the power of love, or the thrill of adventure? These themes and elements can provide profound insights into your innermost desires.

Recognizing Patterns in Your Preferences

Next, let's dive deeper. As you look at your list of favorite stories, begin to recognize patterns. Do you notice recurring themes or character traits that draw you in? Are there particular genres or settings that repeatedly capture your imagination?

For example, if you find that many of your favorite stories involve characters who display unwavering determination in the face of adversity, this might hint at a deep-rooted admiration for resilience and tenacity.

Unveiling Your Inner World

As we explore these patterns and themes in your favorite stories, you'll start to unveil your inner world of passions. The traits and qualities that draw you to these stories might be the very qualities you wish to embody in your own life.

Perhaps your favorite tales involve characters who create change and make the world a better place. This could reveal a latent passion for social impact and change-making.

Or maybe your list is filled with stories of unbreakable friendships and the power of human connections, pointing to a passion for building strong relationships and fostering connections with others.

Bringing Your Passions to Life

The key to living a passionate life is to recognize these patterns and integrate them into your daily existence. You can use the insights gained from your favorite stories to enrich your career, your hobbies, and your relationships.

For example, if you're drawn to stories of scientific discovery, you might find passion in exploring new technologies or scientific innovations. If you love stories of brave heroes who protect the vulnerable, you might seek opportunities to volunteer or work in roles that support the less fortunate.

Your Stories, Your Passions

Remember, your favorite stories are unique to you. They are a window into your soul, offering clues to the passions that can light up your life.

The stories that have touched your heart and stirred your imagination over the years can serve as a guide, illuminating the path toward a more purposeful and passionate existence. They reveal not only what you love but who you are and who you aspire to become.

So, let's embark on this journey into your favorite stories, and in doing so, let's uncover the passions that have been quietly waiting for their moment to shine.

Key Takeaways

- Consider why you love these stories. Is it the hero's journey, the underdog's triumph, or the power of love or adventure? These themes and elements can provide profound insights into your innermost desires.

- Recognize patterns in your preferences. Do you notice recurring themes, character traits, genres, or settings that draw you in? These patterns could reveal qualities and passions you wish to embody in your own life.

- Your favorite stories are unique to you and offer clues to the passions that can light up your life. They reveal not only what you love but who you are and who you aspire to become. Embrace them as a guide to a more meaningful existence.

CHAPTER THIRTEEN

CRAFTING YOUR LEGACY

In the grand tapestry of existence, the notion of leaving a legacy often seems reserved for the famous, influential, or those who make headlines. But let me assure you that our legacy is not limited to the glittering figures that adorn history books. Each of us has the power to shape and craft our legacy in ways that are deeply personal, meaningful, and resounding.

What's Your Legacy?

Before you can begin shaping your legacy, you must first understand what legacy means to you. Legacy is not just a mark you leave on the world; it's a testament to the impact you wish to make. This chapter will guide you in considering how you want to be remembered, not by the masses, but by those whose lives you touch.

So, what's your legacy? It's not about the grandeur of wealth or fame; it's about the character, values, and actions you wish to imprint on the world. Legacy is about the positive ripples that extend outward from your existence.

Legacy Lessons from the Unfamous

To grasp the full extent of legacy's reach, we'll first journey into the lives of ordinary people who, despite not gracing the covers of magazines or occupying center stage, have crafted the most extraordinary legacies.

Consider the schoolteacher who instilled a love of learning in generations of students, the uncelebrated neighbor who silently helped those in need or the unsung mentor who ignited the spark of ambition in countless hearts. These individuals remind us that legacy knows no fame, only purpose.

Highlighting Your Most Important Goals

Legacy is not a distant promise; it's built from the fabric of your everyday actions and choices. To create a legacy that resonates with your passions, you must identify your most important goals.

What are the things you genuinely care about? What are the causes that tug at your heartstrings? What are the contributions you yearn to make to your community, your loved ones, and the world?

Your legacy is the sum of the goals you set and achieve, the lives you touch, and the difference you make. It's a mosaic formed by the pieces of your passions, kindness, and actions.

Consider the following to inspire you on what your legacy could be:

- How can you use your unique talents and skills to contribute to a cause you're passionate about?

- What actions can you take today to make the world a better place, even if only in a small corner of it?

- Who are the people in your life you wish to inspire, encourage, or support?

Remember, legacy is not defined by the accolades and praise of strangers but by the genuine gratitude and admiration of those who know you well.

Your Most Significant Achievements

As you ponder your legacy, take a few moments to envision the future. Picture the impact you wish to have in the coming year, the next five years, and beyond.

What will be your most significant achievements on this journey? Will it be the mentorship you provide, the community projects you lead, or the love and care you share with your family?

Identify at least three key achievements you wish to highlight in your life's narrative. Let them be meaningful, significant, and a testament to your passions.

The Power of Purposeful Living

The path to crafting your legacy is illuminated by purposeful living. By understanding your passions, setting meaningful goals, and committing to action, you transform the nebulous idea of legacy into a tangible reality.

Remember, legacy is not only for the famous. It's for all who dare to live with intention and to leave the world a little better than they found it.

So, let's embark on this journey together, and in doing so, let's create legacies that aren't measured in headlines or fortunes but in the hearts and lives we touch along the way.

Key Takeaways

- Ordinary people who touch lives through their everyday actions teach us that legacy knows no fame, only purpose.

- Identify your most important goals and causes that matter to you. Your legacy is interwoven with your passions, and by highlighting your most meaningful goals, you create a path toward a passionate and impactful life.

- Legacy is defined by the gratitude and admiration of those who know you well, not by accolades from strangers.

- Envision the impact you want to have on the world from the coming year to the next five years and beyond. Identify at least three significant achievements that align with your passions and values.

CHAPTER FOURTEEN

THE COMMON DENOMINATOR

Passions are often like an arrangement of stars, seemingly distant and disconnected at first glance. If you've ever gazed at the stars and tried to spot patterns, you know the feeling of connecting the dots to reveal a familiar shape. Your passions are much the same. You might feel like your interests and enthusiasms are scattered and unrelated, but there's an underlying structure waiting to be discovered.

In this chapter, we will identify the key elements that tie your passions together. Just as constellations share common stars, your passions share common elements, and recognizing these connections can lead to a profound revelation.

Passion's Hidden Thread

Have you ever noticed that you're drawn to seemingly unrelated things in life? You may love painting, hiking, cooking, and coding, and on the surface, these interests appear to have little in common.

However, when you look closely, you'll see that there are threads connecting them together.

For instance, the precision and attention to detail required in painting can be linked to the meticulous problem-solving of coding. Similarly, the sense of adventure experienced through hiking can mirror the creativity and exploration involved in cooking.

Bringing Clarity to Your Journey

Uncovering the common elements of your passions can bring clarity to your journey and help you understand yourself in a new light.

By identifying these core elements, you'll find the unifying themes that excite you and give your life a sense of purpose. For some, it might be the joy of creation; for others, it could be the thrill of discovery or the satisfaction of being helpful.

Your Unique Constellation

Remember, just like a constellation, your passions are unique to you. Nobody else has your exact combination of interests and skills. Embrace your individuality and the beautiful tapestry of passions that make you who you are.

As we explore this concept further, I encourage you to reflect on your passions and the experiences that truly light you up. Look for patterns in what you enjoy doing, even if these activities seem unrelated on the surface. These patterns are the stars in your personal constellation.

For example, you might discover that you're consistently drawn to activities that involve solving complex problems, whether it's creating a gourmet meal or debugging a computer program. This could be a sign that your passion revolves around problem-solving and innovation.

Unlocking The Power of Your Common Denominator

The common elements in your passions can serve as a compass, guiding you toward a more fulfilling life. By recognizing these threads, you can make intentional choices that align with your true desires. They can help you in your career decisions, relationships, and personal development.

Whether you're early in your career, contemplating a shift, or simply seeking a deeper understanding of your life's direction, identifying your common denominator is a powerful tool. Below, I will outline some practical exercises to help you connect the dots between your interests.

Connecting the Dots

We'll start with a simple but revealing exercise that can shed light on the common denominator behind your passions.

Exercise 1: Passion Journal

To identify the key elements that thread through your interests, it's a great idea to start a passion journal. This is your personal canvas for exploring the landscapes of your passions.

1. **Record Your Activities**: Each day, jot down the activities you engaged in and how they made you feel. These activities can be as simple as taking a walk, trying a new recipe, reading a book, or working on a project.

2. **Emotions and Sensations**: Alongside each activity, note the emotions or sensations it evoked. Were you excited, calm, inspired, or challenged? Did it make you lose track of time? These emotional cues are essential to understand.

3. **Patterns and Themes**: Over the course of a week or longer, review your journal. Look for patterns or recurring themes. Do certain emotions or types of activities consistently stand out? These are your initial clues.

4. **Connections**: Try to connect these themes with your passions. How might your love for a specific emotion or sensation relate to your interests?

For example, if you often find solace in nature, a common thread could be a passion for serenity or adventure. If problem-solving consistently excites you, it could be a sign that innovation and critical thinking are central elements of your passions.

Sharing Insights

Once you've explored your passion journal and started to see connections, don't hesitate to share your insights with a trusted friend or mentor. Sometimes, an outside perspective can provide valuable feedback on patterns you might have missed.

Leveraging Your Common Denominator

Your common denominator will offer you a point of reference and guidance. This newfound clarity can empower you in numerous ways:

1. **Career Alignment**: You can align your career choices more closely with your passions. This might mean seeking a job that directly involves the elements that excite you most.

2. **Personal Growth**: Understanding your common denominator can guide your personal growth. You can focus on developing skills and experiences that resonate with your passions.

3. **Improved Relationships**: Recognizing the common threads in your interests can also enhance your relationships. You can

connect with like-minded individuals who share your passions and values.

4. **Legacy Building**: With your passions at the forefront, you can craft a legacy that's meaningful and impactful. Your unique combination of passions is your personal brand, and it can shape the impact you make on the world.

A Journey of Self-Discovery

As we continue on this journey of self-discovery, you'll not only identify your passions but also learn how to leverage them for a more fulfilling life. Your common denominator is a powerful tool, and it's unique to you.

Just like constellations in the night sky, the patterns of your passions form a beautiful and distinct image. Embrace this uniqueness. Celebrate the threads that connect your interests and use them as your compass for a more passionate and purposeful life.

Remember, this journey is a process, and sometimes it takes time to fully grasp your common denominator. Be patient with yourself and enjoy the discovery. Your passions are the stars that light up your life, so let them shine brightly.

Key Takeaways

The hidden threads in your passions might relate to emotions, sensations, or recurring themes. Identifying them can lead you to your common denominator.

Your passions are unique to you, forming a constellation that no one else shares. Embrace your individuality and the beautiful tapestry of passions that make you who you are.

Exercises, like keeping a passion journal, can help you identify the key elements that thread through your interests. Sharing your insights with others can provide valuable feedback.

CHAPTER FIFTEEN

PUTTING YOUR PASSIONS TO WORK

Leveraging Your Passion in Every Aspect of Life

Now that you've uncovered the depths of your passions, it's time to set them in motion. This chapter will be your guide to incorporating your newfound passions into various facets of your life. Whether you're looking to spark change in your career, relationships, or personal development, this is where it all begins.

Turning Passions into Professions

We often hear the advice, "Do what you love, and you'll never work a day in your life." It's not just a catchy phrase; it's a profound truth. Your passions can be your greatest assets in crafting a fulfilling career.

But how do you make the transition from a passion seeker to a passion-driven professional? Let's explore the essential steps to help you find your path.

Step 1: Clarify Your Vision

Turning your passion into a profession starts with a clear vision. Begin by asking yourself these questions:

- **What does a career driven by my passions look like?**

- **What do I want to achieve professionally?**

- **How can my passions benefit others or solve a problem?**

Having a detailed vision will provide you with a destination to aim for.

Step 2: Skill Development

Once you've clarified your vision, identify the skills needed to make your passion a profession. You may already possess some of these skills. Still, it's crucial to continually improve and acquire new ones.

- **Seek out learning opportunities:** Whether through formal education, online courses, or mentorship, invest in your skill development.

- **Practice and refine your skills:** Hands-on experience is invaluable. The more you practice, the better you become.

- **Stay up to date:** It's essential to keep your skills current in rapidly changing fields.

Step 3: Build a Network

Your network is your net worth. The people you connect with can provide guidance, support, and opportunities. Here's how to expand your professional network:

- **Attend industry events:** Conferences, seminars, and workshops are excellent places to meet like-minded individuals.

- **Join online communities:** Social media groups, forums, and professional networking sites can connect you with experts in your field.

- **Seek mentors:** Finding a mentor who's turned their passion into a profession can be incredibly beneficial.

Step 4: Create a Portfolio

Whether you're an artist, writer, entrepreneur, or any other professional, a portfolio showcases your work. It's a testament to your skills and dedication.

- **Include your best work:** Select pieces or projects that highlight your abilities.

- **Update it regularly:** As you grow, your portfolio should reflect your progress.

Step 5: Seek Opportunities

As your skills grow and your network expands, look for opportunities to turn your passion into a profession.

- **Freelancing:** Offer your services to individuals or companies that align with your passions.

- **Entrepreneurship:** If your passion involves solving a problem or meeting a need, consider starting your own venture.

- **Career Change:** Explore job opportunities that allow you to pursue your passion professionally.

Step 6: Perseverance

The path from passion to profession is rarely without hurdles. Rejections, setbacks, and challenges are part of the journey. In the face of these difficulties, it can be tricky to remain on track. Here's how to stay resilient:

- **Embrace failure:** Use failures as learning opportunities. They often lead to success.

- **Stay committed:** Passion-driven professionals are persistent. Keep working toward your goals, even when it gets tough.

- **Celebrate successes:** No matter how small, acknowledge your achievements along the way.

Step 7: Give Back

Your passion doesn't just benefit you; it can make a positive impact on others. Consider how you can use your expertise to help and inspire others.

- **Mentorship:** Share your knowledge and experience with those starting their journey.

- **Community involvement:** Get involved in initiatives or projects that align with your passions.

Taking the Plunge

The road to turning your passion into a profession is undoubtedly challenging, but it's also incredibly rewarding. Imagine a life where your career aligns with your passions, where each day doesn't feel like work but a journey toward fulfillment.

In these final chapters, we'll examine the specific aspects of leveraging your passions, from cultivating your professional brand to enhancing your relationships and personal growth. By the end, you'll be well on your way to a life where your passions fuel your every step.

Remember, your passions are your guideposts. They not only enrich your life but also those of the people you touch along your journey. So, let's start transforming your passions into a profession that will light up your world.

Key Takeaways

- Passion can be your greatest career asset, making work feel like a labor of love.

- Clarify your vision for a passion-driven career, set professional goals, and focus on how your passions benefit others.

- Give back by mentoring, getting involved in your community, or helping others in ways that align with your passions.

- The path to a passion-driven career is challenging but rewarding, offering a fulfilling and purposeful life. Your passions are your guiding stars on this journey.

CHAPTER SIXTEEN

A PASSIONATE LIFE

Achieving Satisfaction and Fulfillment

As we've discussed, passions can lead to a life filled with satisfaction and fulfillment. There are many benefits to living a passionate life, and it has the potential to transform your overall well-being. While the pursuit of passion is often associated with excitement and a burning desire to achieve, it's also a path to profound peace. Living a passionate life goes beyond the thrill of the chase; it brings a deep sense of harmony and contentment.

Let's conclude by pulling everything together and observing how this peace can permeate every corner of your existence.

Passion as a Source of Inner Peace

Passion isn't just a fleeting emotion; it's a powerful force that can lead to a state of inner tranquility. When you're in sync with your passions, it can feel like all the conflicting elements of your life are

64

harmonizing into a beautiful symphony. Here's how passion becomes a source of inner peace:

1. **Alignment with Purpose:** Your passions are often intertwined with your purpose. When you're living in alignment with your purpose, a profound sense of fulfillment washes over you.

2. **Reduced Stress:** Engaging in activities and pursuits you're passionate about can significantly reduce stress. The worries of the day seem to fade into insignificance when you're immersed in your passions.

3. **Timelessness:** Have you ever been so engrossed in an activity that time seems to stand still? This state of flow, often associated with passion, is a gateway to a timeless and peaceful experience.

4. **Clarity and Focus:** Passion can sharpen your focus. When you're passionate about something, your mind naturally becomes clear, and you can concentrate on the task at hand. This focus is a gateway to inner calm.

5. **Resilience:** Passionate individuals tend to be more resilient. When you're pursuing something you deeply care about, setbacks become stepping stones, not stumbling blocks. This resilience contributes to your overall peace of mind.

Fulfillment in Every Aspect of Life

A passionate life doesn't mean just one aspect of your existence is transformed. It ripples through your career, relationships, personal development, and beyond. Let's explore how living with passion can lead to fulfillment in these areas:

1. **Career Fulfillment:** When your career aligns with your passions, work doesn't feel like a burden. It becomes an extension of your

interests and values, leading to career satisfaction.

2. **Relationship Enrichment:** Passion often extends to your relationships. Being passionate about your spouse, significant other, family, and friends can deepen your connections and bring joy to your interactions.

3. **Personal Growth:** Passion fuels personal growth. It propels you to learn, evolve, and become the best version of yourself, contributing to a sense of accomplishment and fulfillment.

4. **Health and Well-being:** Passion can positively impact your health. Pursuing physical activities or dietary habits you're passionate about can lead to a healthier, more vibrant life.

5. **Creativity and Innovation:** Passion is a wellspring of creativity. When you're passionate about something, your mind is more open to innovation and novel solutions to problems.

Balancing Your Passions

Living a passionate life doesn't mean diving headfirst into one pursuit and ignoring everything. It's about balance, like orchestrating a beautiful symphony where each instrument has its place. Here's how you can balance your passions:

1. **Prioritizing:** Acknowledge that not all your passions are equal. Some might be your life's central theme, while others play supporting roles. Prioritize your passions, giving more time and energy to those that are closest to your heart.

2. **Time Management:** Carefully allocate time to your various passions. You may dedicate a few hours each day or specific days of the week to different pursuits. Effective time management ensures none of your passions are neglected.

3. **Cross-Pollination:** Sometimes, your passions can complement one another. For instance, your love for music might enhance your painting, or your passion for cooking could be a creative outlet for sharing meals with friends. Seek opportunities for these passions to cross-pollinate.

4. **Boundaries:** Setting boundaries is crucial to avoid burnout. Understand your limits and be mindful not to overcommit. It's essential to pursue your passions without letting them become a source of stress.

The Journey to a Passionate Life

Embracing a passionate life is a process. It's not always a smooth ride, and challenges may arise along the way. However, the journey itself is immensely rewarding. Here's how you can navigate this path with grace:

1. **Self-Discovery:** Continuously explore and discover new aspects of yourself. Your passions may evolve over time, so stay open to change.

2. **Courage:** Pursuing your passions often requires courage. You might have to step out of your comfort zone, face criticism, or take risks. Embrace these challenges as opportunities for growth.

3. **Community:** Surround yourself with like-minded individuals who share your passions. Building a supportive community can provide encouragement, inspiration, and a sense of belonging.

4. **Resilience:** Understand that setbacks are part of the journey. Instead of seeing them as failures, view them as valuable lessons that propel you forward.

5. **Gratitude:** Practice gratitude for the ability to pursue your passions. It's a powerful tool to maintain a positive mindset and overcome obstacles.

A Life of Abundance

A passionate life is, by nature, a life of abundance. It's abundant in joy, fulfillment, and the richness of experience. It's not about amassing material wealth but about cultivating the wealth of the soul.

As you traverse this path, remember that the pursuit of passion is a lifelong endeavor. Your passions will ebb and flow, and the landscape of your life will evolve. Embrace this ever-changing journey with an open heart, and you'll find that the peace and contentment it brings can be profoundly transformative.

Nurturing Your Passions in Career and Business

Your career and business are often where you spend a significant portion of your waking hours. It's only natural to seek passion and purpose in these areas of life. Let's explore how you can infuse your professional life with passion, turning your daily work into something deeply meaningful and fulfilling.

Choosing the Right Career Path

The first step in bringing passion to your career is choosing the right path. But how do you do this?

1. **Self-Reflection:** Take the time to understand your own strengths, weaknesses, values, and interests. Reflect on the skills that come naturally to you and consider the tasks or projects that make you lose track of time. Your ideal career might be closely tied to these aspects.

2. **Exploration:** Don't be afraid to explore different careers. This might mean taking on internships, volunteering, or even

changing professions. Exploring different options can help you discover what truly excites you.

3. **Alignment with Passions:** Seek out careers that align with your passions. For example, if you're passionate about environmental conservation, a career in sustainability or ecology might be a perfect fit for you.

4. **Education and Skills:** Sometimes, pursuing your passion requires gaining specific skills or qualifications. Be prepared to invest in your education if it opens the door to your dream career.

Infusing Passion into Your Current Job

Not everyone can switch careers but don't worry. It's still possible to find passion in your current job. Here's how:

1. **Micro-Moments of Passion:** Identify tasks within your job that you genuinely enjoy and are passionate about. These could be as simple as organizing events, mentoring a colleague, or designing presentations. Find ways to do more of these tasks.

2. **Innovation and Creativity:** Sometimes, passion comes from finding innovative ways to do your job. Think creatively about how you can improve processes or solve problems. Your enthusiasm for these innovations can drive passion.

3. **Leadership and Responsibility:** Seek leadership opportunities within your current job. Whether it's leading a team or taking charge of a project, these roles often come with more autonomy and the chance to infuse your own passion into your work.

Entrepreneurship and Passion-Driven Businesses

If you're an entrepreneur or considering starting your own business, passion can be a driving force. Here's how:

1. **Identify Your Core Passion:** Before launching a business, ask yourself what you're truly passionate about. Your business should align with this core passion. It's this alignment that will provide the motivation to overcome challenges and persevere.

2. **Solving Real Problems:** The most successful businesses often solve real-world problems. Identify a problem that you're passionate about solving and build your business around that.

3. **Building a Supportive Team:** If you're starting a business, surround yourself with a team that shares your passion. This shared enthusiasm can create a vibrant and innovative work environment.

4. **Pivoting and Adapting:** Be open to adapting your business as you learn and grow. Sometimes, your initial business idea might evolve into something even more aligned with your passion.

Balancing Work and Life

While pursuing a passionate career or business is important, it's equally vital to balance work with your personal life and other passions. Finding this balance can help prevent burnout and ensure holistic well-being.

1. **Set Boundaries:** Create clear boundaries between work and personal life. When your workday ends, make an effort to disconnect from work-related tasks and spend quality time with family and friends or pursue other interests.

2. **Time Management:** Effective time management is crucial for balancing your professional and personal passions. Allocate time to each aspect of your life and stick to these schedules as closely as possible.

3. **Self-Care:** Don't neglect self-care. Regular exercise, a healthy diet, and sufficient sleep are essential for maintaining the energy and enthusiasm necessary for pursuing your passions both in and outside of work.

Regardless of whether you're just beginning your career or are a seasoned professional, it's never too late to seek greater fulfillment and meaning in what you do. Passion is a driving force that can lead to not only professional success but also a more satisfying and balanced life.

Key Takeaways

- Passion isn't just excitement; it's a gateway to inner tranquility. Aligning with your purpose, reducing stress, experiencing timelessness, gaining clarity, and building resilience are pathways to finding inner calmness.

- Passion doesn't just impact one area; it enriches your career, relationships, personal growth, health, and creativity. It brings joy, deepens connections, propels learning, enhances well-being, and sparks innovation in diverse aspects of life.

- Living passionately requires balance. Ensure you prioritize, manage time effectively, allow passions to complement each other, and set boundaries to avoid overwhelming yourself. Balance is about orchestrating passions harmoniously.

- Embracing a passionate life involves self-discovery, courage, community, resilience, and gratitude. Understand that setbacks are part of the journey and leverage them as opportunities for growth.

- A passionate life is abundant in experiences, joy, and fulfillment. It's about cultivating the richness of the soul, not just accumulating material wealth.

- Choosing the right career aligned with your passions, infusing passion into your current job, entrepreneurial endeavors, and balancing work-life integration are all feasible approaches to nurturing passion in professional endeavors.

CONCLUSION

In the pursuit of passion, you have embarked on a profound journey of self-discovery. The quest to find purpose and meaning in every corner of your life is a noble endeavor, and as you reach the conclusion of this book, it's important to take stock of your insights and prepare to take action.

Embrace Your Journey

Your exploration of passion has likely uncovered an assortment of desires, talents, and aspirations. These are the building blocks of a passionate life. By delving into your willingness to embrace unconventional paths as Angela, Tim, Lily, Maggie, Liam, and Professor Ocean did, you, too, open yourself to new and unexpected passions. It's a reminder that passion is not exclusive to grand pursuits; it resides in the everyday.

The Importance of Sharing

As you continue on your path, consider the significance of sharing your passionate life with others. Your enthusiasm and purpose can inspire those around you. Like ripples in a pond, your passion can create a positive impact that extends far beyond your own life. By sharing your journey and discoveries, you become a beacon of possibility for others.

The world is hungry for individuals who have found their passion, for they are the ones who can ignite change, inspire progress, and breathe life into the mundane. The stories of the unconventional paths that led to transformation from conventional roles are a testament to the incredible power that passion can have in your life.

As you stand at the crossroads of your own journey, remember that this is not the end but the beginning. Embrace your newfound passions, explore the unconventional, and share your experiences with the world. Your passionate life is a gift waiting to be unwrapped, and it has the potential to bring profound satisfaction and fulfillment.

And now, as you close this book, take the first step towards your passionate life. The world awaits the unique impact that only you can make. Your journey to discover your passions has just begun, and with each step, you move closer to solving **The Passion Puzzle**—a life filled with meaning, purpose, and contentment that can only come from living a life you are truly passionate about.

ACKNOWLEDGEMENTS

In the grand tapestry of life, there are moments when we pause to express our deepest gratitude. This book, "The Passion Puzzle: Discovering Your Life's Missing Piece," is one of those moments. It's a moment to recognize and appreciate the many threads that have woven together to create this work.

First and foremost, I want to thank my beloved wife, Talondia. Your unwavering support, patience, and love have been the cornerstone of my life and this book. You are a true inspiration, and your pursuit of passion as the Director of Household Operations has been a guiding light for us all.

To my children, you are my greatest teachers. Your curiosity, innocence, and boundless energy remind me of the importance of finding joy in the simplest of moments. You inspire me to be a better person every day.

To my family, both near and far, you have been the wind beneath my wings. Your encouragement and belief in my journey to crack the passion code have propelled me forward. Your stories and shared experiences have enriched the pages of this book.

To my nieces and nephews, your youthful exuberance and unbridled enthusiasm for life have reminded me of the vitality that passion brings. You are the torchbearers of a brighter future.

To my church members, your unwavering faith and commitment to living a purposeful life have been a source of inspiration. Your stories of resilience and determination have found their way onto these pages.

To the countless others who have shared their stories and insights along this journey, you have added depth and richness to this book. Your collective wisdom has shaped its message and purpose.

I also extend my gratitude to the many authors, thinkers, and creators whose works have inspired me. Your words have been a source of enlightenment and guidance on this path to passion.

To my readers, you are the heartbeat of this book. Your quest for meaning and purpose in life mirrors my own, and it is my deepest hope that the words within these pages will inspire and guide you on your journey.

Finally, to my Lord and Savior Jesus Christ, for conspiring in mysterious ways to bring this book to life, I offer my heartfelt thanks.

This book is a testament to the power of passion, the importance of self-discovery, and the beauty of the human spirit. It is a reminder that within each of us lies a missing piece waiting to be found, a passion waiting to be ignited.

With gratitude and humility,

James Becton

The Passion Puzzle

© Becton Capital Inc.

www.jamesbecton.com

TABLE OF CONTENTS

KNOW
WHAT YOU
WANT

EVALUATE YOUR TRUE WANTS AND PASSIONS

The first step to solving the passion puzzle is to figure out what you really want & what you really care about.

Take time to really consider the following questions. The answers held within may be the **key** that helps **resolve** the passion puzzle.

Don't get stuck if you can't think of enough answers for each section, Also, don't be afraid to list more than required! Feel free to use the same answers for multiple questions. A reoccurring answer may be a sign of your true passion.

Knowing What's Important to You

This section is all about brainstorming to figure out the things that are truly important to you.

Name 3 Things You Would Do if Money Were No Object

1. ____

____

____

2. ____

____

____

3. ____

____

____

Name 3 Jobs/Pursuits That You Would Do If You Didn't Get Paid

1. ____

____

____

2. ____

____

____

3. ____

____

____

**What Type of Things Would You Attempt if You Were
Guaranteed to Succeed**

1. ____

____

____

2. ____

____

____

3. ____

____

____

**What kind of superhero are you? (i.e., what is truly important to
you, what issues/challenges do you feel deeply connected to)**

1. ____

____

____

2. _______________________________________

____

____

3. _______________________________________

____

____

4. _______________________________________

____

____

5. _______________________________________

____

____

6. _______________________________________

____

____

7. _______________________________________

____

____

8. _________________________________

____

____

9. _________________________________

____

____

10. _________________________________

____

____

List Things That Truly Make You Happy

1. _________________________________

____

____

2. _________________________________

____

____

3. _________________________________

____

____

4. ____

____

____

5. ____

____

____

6. ____

____

____

7. ____

____

____

8. ____

____

____

9. ____

____

____

10.____

____

In this section, you will take a look at 3 areas of your life and list the desired outcomes you'd like in each of them.

Make sure you choose specific outcomes that you can actually measure.

Personal Life (Health, Fitness, Relationships, etc....)

1. ____

____

____

2. ____

____

____

3. ____

____

____

Professional Life (Career, Education, Financial, etc....)

1. ____

____

____

2. ____

____

____

3. ____

____

____

Spiritual Life (Faith, Ministry, Mentorship, etc....)

1. ____

____

____

2. ____

____

____

3. ____

____

____

VISUALIZATION AND MEDITATION

U sing the above exercises, you should now have a good idea about the things you both enjoy and feel passionate about.

One way that you can begin to "discover your life's missing piece" is by visualizing your life as if you already have what you want. This type of visualization is used by world-class athletes and high achievers across the world.

91

Take time to write down your ideal life in as specific detail as possible...

Now that you have this picture of your ideal life, the key is to keep it in your mind as much as possible. A great way to do that is to tap into the power of meditation.

Take some time each day to envision your ideal life. This will help you drill down to figure out exactly what you want. Below is a handy chart that you can use to record your thoughts about your session.

Monday *Time Spent Meditating/Visualizing:*

How I Felt During:

____

____

____

How I Felt After:

____

____

____

Tuesday *Time Spent Meditating/Visualizing:*

How I Felt During:

____

____

____

How I Felt After:

____

____

____

Wednesday   *Time Spent Meditating/ Visualizing:*

How I Felt During:

____

____

____

How I Felt After:

____

____

____

Thursday   *Time Spent Meditating/ Visualizing:*

How I Felt During:

____

____

____

How I Felt After:

____

____

____

Friday   *Time Spent Meditating/Visualizing:*

How I Felt During:

____

____

____

How I Felt After:

____

____

____

Saturday   *Time Spent Meditating/Visualizing:*

How I Felt During:

____

____

____

How I Felt After:

____

____

____

Sunday *Time Spent Meditating/Visualizing:*

How I Felt During:

____

____

____

How I Felt After:

____

____

____

KNOW
WHO
YOU ARE

EVALUATING YOUR STRENGTHS & WEAKNESSES

I n the last section, we spent time figuring out what we truly want, and who we truly are. In this section, we keep looking inside ourselves, but this time to figure out the innate skills/talents we already have.

Recognizing Your Strengths

If any of these skills/talents line up with our wants and desires, then that is the perfect place to begin to solve the passion puzzle.

What Are Some Things You Have Always Been Good At?

1. ____

____

____

2. ____

____

____

3. ____

____

____

4. ____

____

____

5. ____

____

____

6. ____

____

____

7. ____

____

____

8. ____

____

____

9. ____

____

____

10.____

____

____

What Do You Do Better Than Anyone Else?

1. ____

____

____

2. ____

____

____

3. ____

____

____

4. ____

____

____

5. ____

____

____

What Do Other People Think Are Your Strengths (ask people if you don't know!)

1. ____

____

____

2. ____

____

____

3. ____

____

____

4. ____

____

____

5. ____

____

____

What Skills Have You Worked on Building During Your Life?

1. ____

____

____

2. ____

____

____

3. ____

____

____

4. ____

____

____

5. ____

____

____

It's important to be aware of your weaknesses so you can determine how to deal with situations where the skill or ability is necessary, but you can't do it.

What Skills Do You Struggle With?

1. ____

____

____

2. ____

____

____

3. ____

____

____

4. ____

____

____

5.

6.

7.

8.

9.

10.

What Tasks Do You Often Procrastinate Doing?

1. ____

____

____

2. ____

____

____

3. ____

____

____

4. ____

____

____

5. ____

____

____

What Do Others See As Your Weaknesses?

1. ____

____

____

2. ____

____

____

3. ____

____

____

4. ____

____

____

5. ____

____

____

What Negative Habits or Personality Traits Do You Suffer From?

1. ____

____

____

2. ____

____

____

3. ____

____

____

4. ____

____

____

5. ____

____

____

6. ______________________________

____

____

7. ______________________________

____

____

8. ______________________________

____

____

Focus on Strengths & Letting Go of Weakness

In this section, we will accomplish two things. First, you will list 3 strengths that you want to double down on and improve. Focusing on your strengths is important because it will make you happier, build your self-esteem and propel you towards your goals.

3 Strengths to Build

1. ____

____

____

2. ____

____

____

3. ____

____

____

Now we will take time to list 3 weaknesses to …let go! Don't beat your head against a wall trying to improve all of your weaknesses. Choose 3 weaknesses that you can simply let go. Accept these weaknesses, love yourself anyways, and think about how you can tackle them in the future while attacking your goals (partnerships, outsourcing, etc....)

1.

I Can Get Around This Weakness By:

____

____

____

2

I Can Get Around This Weakness By:

____

____

____

3.

I Can Get Around This Weakness By:

____

____

____

KNOW
WHAT TO
DO NEXT

COMMITMENT TO PRIORITIES

All the brainstorming, wishing, hoping, self-appraisal & visualization in the world won't help you solve the passion puzzle to reach your goals, unless it is followed by ACTION.

The final step before taking massive action is to choose a few priorities to focus on. In our humble opinion, 1 is probably the place to start, but if you feel super ambitious, we have included space for three.

Choose your top 3 priorities of things you want to change, accomplish or focus on for the next while. Be as specific as possible. Think big picture here.

My Top 3 Priorities

1. ____

____

____

2. ____

____

____

3. ____

____

____

BREAKING IT DOWN

Now that you have three priorities, it is time to create an action plan to attack them. For the purposes of this workbook, we will look at a month-long time frame. The system we are about to show you, can be adjusted to fit a year (or multi-year long) goal as well. The basic idea is to break your **priorities** down into **goals**, and those goals into specific **actions**.

Priority One:

Write Down 3 Goals For This Month That Propel You Towards Your Priority:

1. ____

____

____

2. ____

____

____

3. ____

____

____

Now Break Each of These Goals into Smaller Weekly Tasks:

Goal 1:

1. ____

____

____

2. ____

____

____

3. ____

____

____

4. ____

____

____

Goal 2:

1. ____

____

____

2. ____

____

____

3. ____

____

____

4. ____

____

____

Goal 3:

1. ____

____

____

2. ____

____

____

3. ____

____

____

4. ____

____

____

Priority Two:

Write Down 3 Goals For This Month That Propel You Towards Your Priority:

1. ____

____

____

2. ____

____

____

3. ____

____

____

Now Break Each of These Goals into Smaller Weekly Tasks:

Goal 1:

1. ____

____

____

2. ____

____

____

3. ____

____

____

4. ____

____

____

Goal 2:

1. ____

____

____

2. _______________________________

____

____

3. _______________________________

____

____

4. _______________________________

____

____

Goal 3:

1. _______________________________

____

____

2. _______________________________

____

____

3. _______________________________

____

____

4. ____

____

____

Priority Three:

Write Down 3 Goals For This Month That Propel You Towards Your Priority:

1. ____

____

____

2. ____

____

____

3. ____

____

____

Now Break Each of These Goals into Smaller Weekly Tasks:

Goal 1:

1. ____

____

____

2. ____

____

____

3. ____

____

____

4. ____

____

____

Goal 2:

1. ____

____

____

2. ____

____

____

3. ____

____

____

4. ____

____

____

Goal 3:

1. ____

____

____

2. ____

____

____

3. ____

____

____

4. ____

____

____

Do you realize what you have just accomplished? You have basically mapped out your entire next month with the sole purpose of "discovering your life's missing piece". The above system of breaking your **priorities** into **goals**, and those **goals** into **tasks**, isn't new but it IS powerful.

You can adjust this system to any time frame you want. You can even drill down further and break up your weekly **tasks** into bite-sized **daily to-dos.** You will be directly mapping out your path to solving the passion puzzle.

This workbook has walked you through figuring out **what you want**, to figuring out **who you are**, and finally has given you a blueprint about **what to do when it** comes to solving the passion puzzle**.**

Thanks for reading all of our material, and I really hope this guide and workbook will help you reach the heights that only those who **discover their life's missing piece** can.